σοφία WISDOM חוכמה

σοφία WISDOM חוכמה

σοφία

WISDOM

חוכמה

σοφία   WISDOM   חוכמה

Wisdom, by Jabez L. Van Cleef
Copyright 2019
Published 2019 at Madison, New Jersey
ISBN: 9781690818212

σοφία   W I S D O M   חוכמה

Chapter 1. 13
Chapter 2 19
Chapter 3. 25
Chapter 4. 29
Chapter 5. 33
Chapter 6. 41
Chapter 7. 47
Chapter 8. 55
Chapter 9. 61
Chapter 10. 65
Chapter 11. 71
Chapter 12. 77
Chapter 13. 83
Chapter 14. 89
Chapter 15. 97
Chapter 16. 103
Chapter 17. 111
Chapter 18. 117
Chapter 19. 125

σοφία   WISDOM   חוכמה

σοφία   WISDOM   חוכמה

Introduction.

The common definition of wisdom calls for an accrued combination of prior knowledge (experiential learning) which is expediently applied to life situations, in order to obtain a proper or desired outcome, or perhaps an understanding. The outcome should be in accord with physical truth without reliance on magic or other suppositions of irrational causation. The truth of the description of such an account should always (to an allowable degree) take into account the inaccuracies inherent in any human perception, as well as the deficiencies of language as a vehicle for portraying events in what is claimed to be a truthful manner. My personal belief is that absolute truth so expressed is not possible, particularly if we consider the various interpretations introduced by the subjective minds of the audience.

There is an atmosphere of impending doom, or at the least, massive paradigm change, in the book of Wisdom, which I have used as the source for my own extended

σοφία W I S D O M חוכמה

verse paraphrase. The anonymous author of the book lived in Egypt in the last century of antiquity (the first century B.C.) Although this person was Jewish, she (or he) did not join the Exodus to Palestine, but rather stayed nearby the finest available library, in Alexandria, and assumed the persona of the wisest Jewish king (Solomon) in order to compose a paean of praise for Wisdom, personified as a woman. In the process she created a commentary on the human quest for justice and the true nature of the human condition. Some people think the book is not pessimistic, but I do not agree; I think rather that the author's choice to write a book with such an unclear outcome both condemns us to, and redeems us from, the dog's life. The original book was written in Greek, and after being translated into Latin, was made part of the bible used by the Roman Catholic Church. In that compendium, the book found itself relegated to an ambiguous section known as the Apocrypha, consisting of books that were considered at that time to be of dubious authorship, or which might contain subject matter that was considered suspicious or questionable, for various reasons. As the centuries passed, most bibles

σοφία   WISDOM   חוכמה

stopped including books of the Apocrypha altogether.

It is my conjecture that the Book of Wisdom was given short shrift because it contains more than a little of the truth. Truth always questions the other things that lie alongside it in the same bed. For instance, the wisdom tradition comes closer than any other part of the Judeo-Christian enterprise to preserving the worship of a woman-figure, as must have been done for many centuries before the preservation in writing of the story of Adam and Eve. Here we have a woman who stands beside God as combined lover, companion, assistant and spokesperson; and we must imagine that her prominence (and her provenance) were found deeply offensive by the sour-tempered men from Asia Minor who met to assemble the biblical canon. And others, who later decided to discard her.

I prefer to regard the author of the book as a real woman, not an imagined one, who takes on the persona of King Solomon as a way of reifying the voice of truth and justice with greater universality.

σοφία WISDOM חוכמה

σοφία   W I S D O M   ח ו כ מ ה

The world is too much with us; late and soon,
Getting and spending, we lay waste our powers…

--William Wordsworth

σοφία WISDOM חוכמה

σοφία   W I S D O M   חוכמה

Chapter 1.

The relation of Wisdom to justice and truth, and how we must always avoid loose speech and falsehood.

Love justice, all you that presume

To judge this earth we call our home.

Perceive your God in the right way,

And seek God in simplicity,

And know God as your good intent,

As your own heart knows what is meant.

For any soul embraces God

Who does not tempt reprisal's rod.

God comes to them that show good faith.

Perversely trace a wand'ring path,

And you will separate from God:

For godly pow'r, when 'tis so tried,

Reproves the unwise with no guide,

And Wisdom will not enter in

Malicious souls awash in sin,

σοφία   WISDOM   חוכמה

Nor will she ever come to dwell
In bodies subject to the thrall
Of lingering sin's persistent call.
The spirit of discipline thus flees
From crass deceit and all its ways,
From thoughts suspended by the trance
Of brute desire and ignorance,
Without the understanding's grace;
And God abandons every place
Where iniquity comes to dwell.
Where God abandons, that is hell.
Holy Wisdom is a spirit
Just and pure, benevolent;
She'll not acquit the careless lapse,
The words that merely drop from lips:
For God is witness of the inner,
God the true searcher of the sinner,
God hears the sound of the loose tongue
And sees the thought that makes it wrong.
The spirit of God fills all the earth:
And that which holds all things from birth

σοφία WISDOM חוכמה

Knows of the voice still in your head;
So injustice cannot be hid,
And neither shall the consequence:
Bad judgment and its recompense
Pass by, thus feigning innocence.
Time's inquisition shall be done
On thoughts of the ungodly one:
The silence of harsh words shall come
To God, Who dwells beyond all time,
And chastises iniquity.
The sharp ear of God's jealousy
Hears what sinners do or don't say:
That quiet tumult, murmuring,
Shall not be hid for anything.
Keep you therefore from slithering speech,
Which profits nothing, cannot teach;
Refrain your tongue from secret thought;
Dark words shall not be heard for nought:
The mouth dissembling kills the soul
Where honest silence keeps it whole.
Seek not death by error of life,

σοφία WISDOM חוכמה

Neither procure the spoils of strife.

God made not death, but by our hands,

Driven by secret thought, life ends.

Neither does God take pleasure in

Wanton destruction of the living.

God made all things that they might be:

And made the nations graciously;

All of the nations of the earth

Were made for health and good and worth.

There is no poison, innate wrath,

In all of these, no force of death;

Upon the earth, no rule of hell,

For justice is perpetual;

For God has made this earth withal,

And God is just, and immortal.

Yet see, the wicked, with works and words,

Have called this world to come to them:

And souls find wickedness a friend,

Following after, to diverse end.

Falsehood makes covenant with them

Because they share the same vile dream:

σοφία WISDOM חוכמה

Of this, to place death before love,
And be some portion evil thereof.

Ω

σοφία WISDOM חוכמה

σοφία   W I S D O M   חוכמה

Chapter 2.

On the wickedness of the ungodly and their original accusations against the righteous.

The wicked would themselves persuade,
Not rightly, but with fearless pride,
That this, the time of human life
Is short and tedious, filled with strife.
And in the end of such a span,
There is no cure for woman or man,
And no one ever has been known
To have returned when life is done.
For out of nothing we are born,
And after, as if we had not been:
In our nostrils the breath we take
Is gone like mist upon a lake,
Our speech a spark of transient light,
To move our heart or share our spite,
Which being put out, our bodies fail,
To soot and ash they fall, so frail,
Poured out abroad as soft as air,
Yet life shall not be anywhere.

σοφία   WISDOM   חוכמה

We shall be as a trace of spray
Dispersed as mist, then driven away,
Overpowered by beams of the sun,
By heat thereof made to be gone.
Our name in time shall be forgot,
And none shall have even a jot,
Any remembrance, in the haze
Of all our works and all our days.
Our time is as a shadow's flight;
Its errors cannot be set right,
There is no going back from death,
Our lips fast sealed against more breath,
And no thing human may return
To living when it's crost the bourne.
Then cries the wicked reveler:
"Come therefore, now let us make cheer
In good things that are present here!
Let us speedily use our flesh
As in our youth when all was fresh,
And fill ourselves with costly wine,
And slick our skins with ointments fine.

σοφία WISDOM חוכמה

Let not the flower of time pass by
But crown ourselves with rose and spray,
Before they wither with the day.

"Let no meadow escape the riot;
Not one shall fail to have a part.
Let luxury be all unbroken,
Let us everywhere leave the token
Of joy and pleasure pulsing hot,
This is our portion, this our lot.
Let us oppress the poor laborer,
And let us not the widow spare,
Nor honor the ancient grey hair
Of all the agèd in their care.
But let our power be the law,
And justice be like the hungry crow,
Searching here and there to eat
Scraps of gristle and dead meat.

"For what is feeble on this earth
Is ever found as nothing worth.

σοφία WISDOM חוכמה

Let us therefore lie here in wait
To snare the just by the front gate.
'Tis not the just from whom we learn,
They restrain us at ev'ry turn;
This one upbraids us for our sin,
And divulges what we have done."
Suffused with pow'r the wicked says:
"The just may boast of all their ways,
That God is always in their eyes;
By claiming to be child of God,
The just now claim to hold the rod,
Be each and all our censurer.
Grievous to us that just one is,
Even to come before our eyes;
His is a life that's not well spent,
And his ways very different.
We are esteemed, costly triflers;
The just abstain from all our ways,
And call them selfish filthiness,
And seek a latter end to bless,
That glories in descent from God.

σοφία WISDOM חוכמה

"Let us then see of this God's child
If time will prove what shall befall,
And we shall know for good or ill
That which shall be our proper end.
For if the just is child of God,
God will surely come to defend
And save this child from evil hands.
Let us examine closely here
By outrage, torture, and raw fear,
That we may know what meekness is,
And try what patience brings to pass.
Let us condemn the just to find
Most shameful death, and make them blind."

And at the end of this dark trial,
God will see the just, and smile.
For they shall take their proper place:
The righteous, standing before God's face.
Respecting all these things they thought,
The wicked were deceived in God's sight;
An unjust malice blinded them,

σοφία WISDOM חוכמה

And they knew not God's secrets then.
Nor did they hope for righteous payment,
For justice, purity or restraint;
Nor praise the honor of holy souls.
For God has made the core of us
Incorruptible, and always was,
The image of what had made us.

But by the envy of the devil,
Death now comes among us all
Into the world while we yet live,
And each of us has pow'r to give
Allegiance to that same evil;
And may take that side, or not at all.

Ω

σοφία   W I S D O M   חוכמה

Chapter 3.

The rewards of just behavior, and the happiness of those who have endured trials.

The souls of the just are in God's hand,
The pain of death shall not touch them.
To the unwise, they seemed to die,
And their departure was misery;
Their going away, destruction;
But now they are in peace anon.
Though in the sight of those who live
They suffered pains before the grave,
Now we see that their hope is full,
Bright with the light of the immortal.
In lesser things they were denied,
In greater they shall find reward.

This is because God has tried them,
Found the worth at the heart of them,

σοφία   WISDOM   חוכמה

As in the furnace, the flame of fire
Drives off all else, leaving gold pure,
God has proved them so to be pure.
And as an ember from a fire,
God receives them to a new home,
And in good time to this they come.
There all these souls in light shall be:
Purity, shining like stars brightly,
Freely will they run to and fro,
Like sparks among reeds will they go.
They shall judge nations, rule all lands,
Amid God's reign that never ends.

Who trusts in God, understands truth:
They rest in God because of faith,
For love lives on with faith and peace,
And love is the greatest of these.

The wicked shall earn punishment
By their own failure to repent,
For all the justice, so neglected,

σοφία   WISDOM   חוכמה

From God against whom they revolted.
They that reject Wisdom's strait lane
Are unhappy: their hope is vain,
Their labors fruitless, works for nought,
Are empty and devoid of thought.
Their spouses are foolish, children cursed,
The generation of the worst.

Happy will be the barren woman;
The undefiled, that has not known
The bed of sin; in expectation,
She shall bear fruit in visitation
Of holy souls, without damnation.
Happy the eunuch, who lives alone,
Who has not wrought nor shared a sin,
Grasped iniquity with his own hands,
Nor blamed God, nor earned reprimands.
The precious gift of faith giv'n him,
Betokens the brighter world to come.
For maid and man the fruit that grows
Is glorious as their labor shows;

σοφία   WISDOM   חוכמה

The root of Wisdom never fails.
But the adult'rers' daughter and son
Must rectify what has been done,
Grow the seed of a lawless bed
Into a just and righteous head.
Else they live long, they shall be seen
As nothing worth, a thing unclean,
And in their old age have no fame;
If they die quickly, they die in shame.
They have no hope lest they repair,
Nor words of comfort in despair,
For dreadful is the consequence,
The leavings of a wicked race.

Ω

σοφία   WISDOM   חוכמה

Chapter 4.

The nature of chastity and innocence.

O how beautiful are the chaste
Clothed in glory, by Wisdom graced.
For their memory lives forever:
Seen and known, forgotten never.
To God and human generations
They offer up their aspirations,
Knowing when purity is fit,
When it is present, preserving it:
Desiring it when it has gone,
And when it triumphs, wear the crown,
Winning the reward and yield
Of conflicts ever undefiled.

But lo! The pestilential grove
Of the wicked shall never thrive,
And bastard slips shall not take root,

σοφία   WISDOM   חוכמה

Nor find a firm spot for the shoot.
And if they flourish for a time
Branching into a sunny clime,
Yet they will not stand upright fast,
They shall be shaken at the last,
With the fresh wind tossing about,
Then they shall all be rooted out.
Then the imperfect branches split,
They shall be broken off of it,
And the tree's fruits shall fall and bruise,
Be sour to eat, too soon to use,
And fit betimes for nothing good;
For all the children of this wood,
Born of these trees, are witnesses
Of sin their parents would possess.

But the just person, standing firm,
If prevented by death's pale worm,
Shall be at rest in spite of this,
For venerable old age is
Not that of long time on this earth,

σοφία WISDOM חוכמה

Nor counted by some years since birth.
Rather understanding appears
In the experience of short years.
A spotless life without sin's wage
Yields up the worthiness of age.
Such lives please God and are beloved;
They are translated as they lived,
They know no death, are taken away
Straight to heaven at the mid-day,
Lest wickedness catch them in toils
Or curved deceit beguile their souls.
For bewitching of vanity
Obscures such good things as it may;
And wandering concupiscence
Beclouds the mind of innocence.
Being made perfect in a short space,
They filled a longer time with grace.
For as their souls pleased God above,
Therefore God hastes to share their love,
Bringing them forth to share a place
Far from the threat of iniquities. Ω

σοφία WISDOM חוכמה

σοφία   WISDOM   חוכמה

Chapter 5.

Wherein we compare the fates of the just and the unjust.

This way of God people may see,
And not yet perceive a Deity;
They lay not up things in their hearts,
And know not where God's mercy starts;
The grace of God that never ends,
And mercy of the saints God sends.
The ones God may have sought to own;
The just, that are now dead and gone.

And God condemns the wicked crowd
That are yet living, long and loud,
While death soon took the virtuous,
Long is the life of the unjust.
For sinners shall see the end arrive
For those wise souls who ought to live,
And shall not understand nor deem
Why virtue did not shelter them,

σοφία WISDOM חוכמה

Why God ordained this fate for them;

Nor why God kept the unjust safe,

Prolonging so their span of life.

The wicked see, and shall despise:

But God shall laugh at all their lies.

The unjust fall without honor;

Shamed among the dead, for ever;

For God shall burst them open wide,

Puffed up and speechless, in their pride;

And God shall shake them hard and fast;

They shall be utterly laid waste:

They shall linger in their sorrow,

Their memory will pass tomorrow.

The unjust, overcome with fear,

See their own sins, bright and clear:

All their iniquities will come

And stand accusing against them.

Then shall the just find constancy

Against all those that took away

Their righteous labors and rewards.

And they, seeing this, shall have no words,

σοφία   WISDOM   חוכמה

They will succumb to sudden fear,
Amazed to see how safe they are,
And smitten by the sharp vision
Of an unexpected salvation.

The proud will say, within themselves,
Repenting, and groaning great sighs
For anguish of the very spirit:
"These are they, now righteous and just,
Whom we all held for some time past
As a parable of reproach.
We looked down on them, all and each;
We fools esteemed their lives to be
Madness, and unworthy to see;
And at their end, without honor.
But behold now, see how they are:
Children of God, the fruit of faith;
While we have left the way of truth,
Where light of justice does not shine;
They walk among the saints above,
Basking in everlasting love;

σοφία   WISDOM   חוכמה

While the sun's understanding rays
Have not yet risen over us.
We bathed ourselves in vats of lust,
Sucked the tip of iniquity's breast;
Of destruction we wrought our days,
As we toiled on through the hard ways:
The way of the Lord we have not known.
So, what for us has our pride done?
What gain, beyond what may be bought,
Has boasting of our riches brought?
All of those things we thought to own
Are passed away like a shadow, gone;
Like the post that casts it thereon;
Or like a ship that passes by,
Through the dark waves so wild and high,
Whereof when it is gone and done,
No trace can e'er be found, not one.
There is no footprint of its keel
As in the treach'rous waters steal;
As when a bird flies through the air,
It leaves the blue sky blank and bare;

σοφία WISDOM חוכמה

Only the sound of the beating wings
Lingers in the sharp ear, and clings;
A sound of bird in air, parting it
By the very force of her flight;
She beats her wings, now here, now there,
And has flown on through summer air,
And there is not a mark or line
Found afterwards where she has been;
As when the arrow its target sees,
The air divides to let it pass;
Then comes the air together again,
So that its passage is not known;
So also, being born are we:
Living, forthwith we cease to be,
And have been able to show no mark
Of virtue, howsoever we work;
But are consumed in our wickedness.
Such things as these we may express
As sinners may well say in hell:
The hope of the wicked is as dust,
Blown abroad by the windy gust;

σοφία WISDOM חוכמה

As a thin froth dispersed by storm,
Or smoke that's scattered without form;
Or as your remembrance of a guest
That stopped by one chill night to rest."

The just shall live for evermore:
And their reward is with the Lord,
The care of them with the most High.
Therefore the just shall shine in glory,
Crowns of beauty to them will come,
God's strong right hand will cover them,
God's holy arm will defend them.
Zeal will take armor, sword and spear
Protecting the creature born to wear
Justice as breastplate, polished clear.
The truth of justice protects the soul
Better than helmet made of steel.
Take now equity's transparent armor
For an invincible shield in war;
And make severest wrath your spear,
And the whole world will then know fear.

σοφία WISDOM חוכמה

So shall you fight against the unwise:
As shafts of lightning fall from the skies;
Falling from clouds as from bow well bent,
They shall be shot out and not relent,
And every one will fly to the mark,
As thick hail comes to do its work:
Ice cast upon the burning earth,
Joining the hot stones in their wrath.
The waters of the sea shall burst
Against the wicked and unjust,
And the rivers, running together,
Rise up to bathe the land in terror.
A mighty wind shall stand against them,
And as a whirlwind shall divide them:
And they, in their iniquity,
Shall bring the earth to ruin that day,
And wickedness shall overthrow
The palaces where the mighty go.

Ω

σοφία WISDOM חוכמה

σοφία   WISDOM   חוכמה

Chapter 6.

The fate and punishment of those who choose to live without Wisdom.

Wisdom over strength may yet prevail;
So a wise person, for good or ill,
May be judged, at the end of all things,
Better by God than all the world's kings.
Hear, O ye heirs of privilege,
Understand; discern, learn, and judge;
You call yourselves better by birth:
Adjudicate now the ends of the earth.

Give ear, attend, all you that rule,
That hold the people in your thrall,
That please yourselves as you process
Before the nations you oppress:
For power is given you by God,
Strength by heaven, not crownèd head.
God will examine the works you do,
Search out your thoughts, and then judge you.
By rule of God's authority,

σοφία WISDOM חוכמה

You have not striven to obey,
Nor kept the law of justice well,
Nor walked according to God's will.
Horribly and speedily
Will God appear before your eye:
For the judgment most severe
Shall be on them that hold the power.
For to the many that are small,
Mercy is giv'n by God's free will;
But the mighty on their great thrones
Will be met with mightier torments.

God will not make an exception
To privilege any one's person,
Neither will God stand in awe
Before rank, or subvert the law:
For God has made both great and little,
And has equally care of all.
Greater punishment sits ready
To rehabilitate the mighty.
To you, therefore, O king and prince,

σοφία WISDOM חוכמה

These are my words, I shall not mince,
That you may learn of holy Wisdom,
And shall not from it lapse and roam:
If you have kept to just things justly,
You shall be justified in your way.
You that have truly learned these things,
Shall find what meaning rests on kings.
Mark therefore this declaration,
Love these words, and have instruction.
Wisdom is glorious, and never fades,
By them that love her, she abides.
She is found by them that seek her.
She waits on them that covet her,
So she may first to them appear
Who wake early to search for her.
The one who seeks shall not labor:
For he shall find her at his door.

Thinking therefore upon Wisdom
Makes perfect understanding come:
And all of them that watch for her,

σοφία WISDOM חוכמה

Shall quickly find themselves secure;
For she goes about the world's border,
Seeking all those worthy of her,
And shows herself to each of them;
She cheers them in the ways they roam,
And meets them with all providence,
Generously answ'ring their plaints.

For the beginning of Wisdom is
The true desire of holy rules.
The care of discipline is love:
Love is the keeping of her laws:
Keeping her laws the firm foundation
To build a house of incorruption:
And incorruption the road to God.
Therefore it is desire of Wisdom
Brings them to th'eternal kingdom.
If you delight in thrones, and scepters,
O kings and queens, and your retainers,
Leave all these for a truer lover;
Love Wisdom, that you may reign for ever.

σοφία WISDOM חוכמה

What Wisdom is, her origin,
I will declare to you again.
I will not hide from you the word
That tells the mysteries of God;
Together we will seek her out
From the beginning of her birth,
And bring the knowledge of her path
To light, and not evade the truth;
I go not with consuming envy,
But keep my whole desire before me,
For if I look at other things,
Wisdom makes me no offerings.

Wisdom amongst the multitude
Is the welfare of the whole world:
Of these my words, let nothing fall,
And she shall profit you full well.

Ω

σοφία   WISDOM   חוכמה

σοφία   WISDOM   חוכמה

Chapter 7.

How Wisdom came into being, told by a king who knew her ways.

> I am mortal, like any other,
>   And in the womb of my mother
> I am as them that were first made
> Of earth, mingled with light and shade;
> I was then formed in the image of God.
> Then I was compacted in blood,
>   The seed of man, the womb of woman,
>   And the pleasure of sleep concurring.

> But then I left my mother's womb;
> My term complete, forth must I come,
> And being born drew common air,
> And fell to earth and lay me there,
> And the first voice which I there knew,
> Was crying, as all others do.
> I was nursed in swaddling clothes,
>   And with great cares and endless woes.

σοφία   WISDOM   חכמה

For none of the royalty on earth
Had any other beginning of birth.
All have one entrance to this place,
And the departure is likewise.

Wherefore a good child I wished to be,
And understanding was given me:
I called on God for help that day,
A spirit of Wisdom came upon me:
And I preferred her thoughts and ways,
Before kingdoms and thrones, and toys.
And I esteemed riches nothing,
In comparison of her everything.

I cannot compare her to precious stone.
Imagine how this pairing is done:
Held side by side in my own hand,
All gems by her are a little sand,
Gold like mud from a tidal bay,
And silver by her counted as clay.
I loved her above health and beauty,

σοφία   WISDOM   חוכמה

Made mindfulness of her my duty,
So I chose her instead of light:
For her light cannot be put out.

Now all these good things came to me
In her train, and out through her eye,
Riches innumerable through her hands,
Goodness of things, that never ends.
And I rejoiced in all of these things
For Wisdom went before me, on wings;
Still I knew of her, there was no other,
Yet of them all she was the mother.

I have learned this without any guile,
Communicate without envy, to all;
And Wisdom's riches I hide not.

For she is treasure infinite!
Which they that spend, make friends with God,
And are commended every day
For gifts of discipline they display.

σοφία   WISDOM   חוכמה

Now God has given to me to speak,
And conceive thoughts worthy alike,
Those things that have been given me:
Because God guides in Wisdom's way,
And God directs the step of the wise:
For in God's hand are this, which is:
We, and our words, and all we mean,
And all the knowledge and skill therein.

For God has given me thus far
True knowledge of the things that are:
To know all that there is to know,
And see of virtues where they go;
Beginnings, ends, and midst of times,
The alterations of their lines,
The change and character of seasons,
The year as made of revolutions,
The dispositions of the stars,
The natures of all living creatures,
Rage of wild beasts and force of winds,
Reasonings of human minds,

σοφία WISDOM חוכמה

Diversities of plants and soils,
Virtues of roots, stems and tendrils,
All things hid and not foreseen,
What they are and what they mean:
Wisdom who works all things that be,
With energy and compassion, taught me.

In her is the spirit of understanding:
Holy, one, manifold, subtle,
Eloquent, active, undefiled, sure,
Sweet, loving that which is good, quick,
Which nothing hinders, beneficent,
Gentle, kind, steadfast, assured,
Secure, having all power, inquiring,
Overseeing all things, containing all spirits,
Intelligible, pure, and subtle.

Wisdom is more active than all activity:
She reaches everywhere with her purity.
For she is a vapor of God's power,
A certain pure emanation and flower,

σοφία   WISDOM   חוכמה

An aura of the expanding glory
Of the almighty God: and therefore
No defilement comes into her.

She is the brightness of eternal light,
The unspotted mirror of God's delight,
The image of the goodness of God
In which no part of the world is hid.

She does all things, yet being but one,
Remaining herself when she is done,
She renews herself into holy minds;
God and prophet she calls her friends.

For God loves nothing better than
The person who dwells with Wisdom.

She is more beautiful than the sun,
Above all orders of stars may her path run:
Compared with light of star or sun,
She is the superior one.

σοφία   WISDOM   חוכמה

> For after the light of day comes night,
> But no evil can overcome Wisdom.
>
> She reaches therefore from end to end
> And all things sweetly take her command.

Ω

σοφία WISDOM חוכמה

σοφία   WISDOM   חוכמה

Chapter 8.

*The same king tells how he loved Wisdom
and reveals the beginning of his own self-delusion.*

I have loved her, and have sought her,

From my youth I have desired her

I became a lover of her beauty.

I followed her beautiful way.

I sought to take her for my spouse,

And live together in my house.

She glorifies her noble word

By holding her converse with God:

The God of all that I may know,

The God who loves her as I do.

She teaches the knowledge of God;

She chooses the works of God.

And if of riches you may dream,

What then is richer than Wisdom?

If senses are made to do work,

Who could be more the artful worker?

She knows those things that spur the sense

To pleasures, ever more intense.

σοφία WISDOM חוכמה

And if a soul revels in justice
Her labors offer greater virtues;
For she teaches justice, and prudence,
And fortitude, and temperance,
And all such things as make us
Needful of nothing that is.

And if a person desires learning
Wisdom knows things past knowing,
Wisdom judges of things to come:
She knows the subtleties of claim,
And the solutions of arguments:
She beholds signs and portents,
And deeds, before they have come to pass,
The events of all times and ages.

She I chose, therefore, to espouse,
To bring her with me to my own house:
Knowing that she will speak to me,
And bring comfort in my misery
And yield in place of weeping, joy.

σοφία   WISDOM   חוכמה

So for her sake I shall have glory
Among the many who hear of me;
Even the ancients will hear of me;
Though they were dead before I was born,
From age to age was our glory foreseen.

I shall be found by past and present
To own a quick conceit in judgment,
And be admired by all the mighty;
The wide eyes of princes shall wonder at me.

They all shall wait on my presence
When I keep silence and hold my peace;
Then look upon me when I speak,
And if I speak at length to them,
Shall place their hands over their mouths.

By means of Wisdom I shall have
Immortality; my thoughts will live
Forever; I will leave behind me
An everlasting memory

σοφία   WISDOM   חוכמה

For them that will come after me.
The peculiar, unique reality
Of thoughts I will leave behind me
Shall set the people in order:
All nations shall be subject to me
Without knowing whence comes their awe.

Terrible rulers hearing her ideas
Shall fear me and mend their ways,
To build compassion out of terror;
The multitude will call me savior
And I shall inspire the valiant in war.

When she and I go into my house,
At her side I shall find repose,
Her speech will have no bitterness,
Nor her company tediousness,
But completion of joy and gladness.

Thinking these things for my own part,
And pondering them in my heart,

σοφία　WISDOM　חוכמה

I have come to see that my tie
To Wisdom is my immortality.
For while I may find delight within me
As moment to moment we are friends,
And riches in the works of her hands;
In the exercise of conference with her
I find eternity, the essence of forever,
A pure moment like flight of birds,
In the expressions of her words.
I had gone about seeking a thought,
That I might know Wisdom complete.
Know this: I was a witty child
And I inherited a good soul;
And I was even more than good,
For I came to a body undefiled.
And as I knew that I could not
Otherwise be of a pure habit,
Except if God gave me this rare gift,
This also showed me Wisdom's point
That I might know whose gift it was:
I went then to beseech the Lord,

σοφία   WISDOM   חוכמה

And I besought with this my word,
Saying with my whole heart this prayer:
As you may read, the next chapter.

Ω

σοφία   WISDOM   חוכמה

Chapter 9.

*The king supposes praise for Wisdom in a hymn,
and senses his own limitations.*

God of my fathers, and my mothers,

Who has made all things, and others,

And by your Wisdom unearthed the human,

That they should seek to have dominion

Over the creatures made by your hand,

That they should try to order the world

According to knowledge and equity,

And serve justice with a steady heart;

God, give me Wisdom, that sits by your throne,

Cast me not off from among your children:

For I am your servant, striving for good,

And the offspring of your handmaid;

A weak person, and of little time,

Falling short in allowing room

For understanding judgment and laws,

And how to help in great and small ways;

For if one is perfect among the children,

Yet if Wisdom is not therein,

σοφία WISDOM חוכמה

That one shall be nothing regarded.
You Lord, chose me to be leader
And a judge of son and daughter.
You Lord, have commanded me
To build a temple before the sky,
An altar to make sacrifice
There, before your dwelling place,
A semblance of the tabernacle,
Which you prepared from the beginning:
And your Wisdom stands beside you,
Who knows your works, and all you do,
Who then also was present when
You made the world for women and men,
And knew what was right in your eyes,
And what follows your holy laws.

Send her out of your holy heaven,
From that majestic, airy throne,
That she may also stand with me,
And may her thoughtful labors ply,
That I may know and thereby do

σοφία WISDOM חוכמה

What is acceptable with you.
For she understands all things that are,
Shall lead me soberly in my labor,
And shall preserve me by her power
Throughout a lifetime, or an hour.

So shall my works hold firm and fast,
And with your people I shall be just,
And show me worthy of the powers
I inherited from my ancestors.

For who can know of God's advice?
Who can think what the will of God is?
The thoughts of mortals are pitiful,
Our counsels unreliable.
Corruptible bodies burden souls,
As earth suppresses my own muse.
And hardly do we guess aright
At things so seen in mortal light.
With labor do we find these things
Within our daily wanderings.

σοφία   WISDOM   חוכמה

But of the things that are in heaven,
Who shall search out, what word is given?
And who on earth shall know your thought,
Save those that your companion sought?
Unless you holy Wisdom give,
And send your spirit from above.
And when the ways of mortal souls
May stand correct by Wisdom's rules,
When all the wounds that we have willed
By Wisdom are made whole and healed,
Whosoever is left standing,
Has pleased thee, God, from the beginning.

Ω

σοφία WISDOM חוכמה

Chapter 10.

*The king tells of how Wisdom sought to reconcile
the just and the unjust.*

When we were created and alone,
First left by God on this cold bourne,
Wisdom preserved us, taught us to live,
Taught us to worship and to love,
And so she brought us out of sin,
And gave us power rightly to govern.

But when the unjust left her side
Seeking in anger to nurture pride,
They perished by their fury, wherein
One would murder another one.
For the cause of the contemptible,
When water turned the earth to rubble,
Wisdom restored the world again,
Sending a message of peace to them,
Redirecting the course of the good
By a vessel of transient wood.

σοφία   WISDOM   חוכמה

When the nations conspired at last
Falling prey to wickedness and lust,
From all of these, she selected the good,
Preserved them without blame to God,
And kept their children strong and safe,
Showing compassion for human life.

She delivered the just, who ran
From the wicked, when fire came down
Upon the city Pentapolis;
Whose land, to mark their wickedness,
Is desolate, and smokes with heat,
And trees bear fruits that ripen not,
And there is a standing pillar of salt,
An incredulous soul's white monument.
Ignoring Wisdom's counsel, they
Lost all their worldly goods that day;
They showed their ignorance of the good,
But left a memory of the bad,
So all they sinned, and all they did,
Could not so much as lie there hid.

σοφία   WISDOM   חוכמה

Thus Wisdom shields from adversity
Them that follow upon her way.

For all the just, she shows this way:
When faced with rank iniquity
She finds the path that leads to God,
She gives the knowledge of what is good,
She makes honorable their labors,
She accomplishes their years,
And if they come, from pride or fate,
To enter into fawning deceit,
She shows them how to stand upright.

She keeps them safe from enemies,
Defends them from a seducer's ways,
And gives them strength to triumph o'er
Whatever obstacles there are.

Because Wisdom, of all the mightiest,
Has never thought to forsake the just:

σοφία   WISDOM   חוכמה

Deliv'ring them from a sinner's lot;
She went down with them into the pit.
She broke their shackles and their chains,
And gave the scepter to One who reigns.
Mighty Wisdom has shown her power
Against all those that oppress the poor;
Revealed the liars that lay in wait,
And everlasting glory brought.

She has delivered all the just,
And the innocent, and the oppressed;
She entered into the soul downtrod
And spoke there as a servant of God,
Against the dreadful kings and queens
And their violent, hidden minions.
She rendered to the just their wage
For toils against the tyrant's rage;
Was covert to them by daylight,
And under shining stars by night:
And she brought them through the Red Sea,
Through a great water showed the way,

σοφία WISDOM חוכמה

And led them out to higher ground,
But their enemies she all drowned.
From depths of hell she brought them out.
Therefore the spoils came to the just.

They sang to your holy name, O God,
And they praised you with one accord.

For Wisdom opened the mouth of the mute,
Made tongues of infants eloquent.

Ω

σοφία WISDOM חוכמה

σοφία WISDOM חוכמה

Chapter 11.

*The king's nation, claiming kinship with their god,
contest with their enemies in the wilderness.*

> They went out through the wilderness;
> They saw the uninhabited place;
> In the sand where they pitched their tents,
> They stood against their enemies.

> When thirst threatened to kill the sick,
> Water was giv'n them from the rock,
> Refreshment came from a barren stone;
> Yet when they left, the water was gone.

> For by such things their enemies
> Were punished in that barren place;
> Yet when their water had failed them,
> God's own children still had some.
> The unjust, washed in human blood,
> Were diminished and degraded;
> By God's command they were punished
> For their guilt in murdering infants,

σοφία   WISDOM   חוכמה

While the just received water abundant,
Restored in strength, and defiant.

You, O God , admonished and tried
Your people, with mercy chastised them;
You showed them how the wicked
Came to be judged and tormented.
For whether absent or present,
All the wicked got the same torment;
The double affliction held them fast:
A groaning for memory of things past.

When the enemy heard from their pains
Others were strengthened and made gains,
They remembered the intent of God,
Wondering, in the end, at what happened.
From these people they scorned before,
The ones thrown out and left to suffer,
When all of them were expected to perish,
They admired only one, in the end.
And the unjust saw this come to pass,

σοφία WISDOM חוכמה

Their thirsting, unlike that of the just,
The foolishness of their iniquity,
Because some had worshipped idols,
Dumb serpents and worthless beasts;
For this you sent a multitudinous
Pestilence of vengeful creatures.
And so they saw the truth in this:

Wherein whatever things we find our sins,
By the same also are we tormented.

For God's almighty munificent hand,
Which made the world of matter profound,
Simultaneous with and without form,
Found certain ways to send upon them
Bears, lions, snakes, and wasps in swarm,
Or unknown beasts of a new kind,
Full of rage, molesting the mind:
Seeming to breathe out fiery spikes,
Or a stinging cloud of stinking smokes,
Or shooting horrible sparks from their eyes:

σοφία   WISDOM   חוכמה

God in these creatures made so wroth,
Made air blood-pink with flying froth;
Whereof not only the hurt might kill
But also the very sight make still
The beating heart within each breast,
And kill them all through fear at last;
Strike them face down upon the dust.

Yes, and even without these beasts,
They might be slain with one great blast,
Persecuted by their own deeds,
And scattered across the barren weeds,
By the breath of relentless power:
But God orders all things in measure,
Measures their fall by number, and weight.
For the greatest power is always so great,
With you alone we may weather this storm,
And who shall resist the strength of your arm?
For the whole world, beside your presence,
Is as the least grain on a balance,
Or as a drop of the morning dew,

σοφία　WISDOM　חוכמה

That falls on the earth when day is new.
But you have mercy upon us all,
For you all things are possible,
You mend or overlook our sins,
And all for the sake of repentance.

For you love all the things that are,
And hate no thing you have made, ever.
For you did not vengefully appoint,
Or make any thing, with hateful intent.

And how could anything endure,
If you would not be there forever?
How even could we be preserved,
If you had not called us to be saved.

Because we are yours, you spare us all,
O God, who so loves every soul.

Ω

σοφία WISDOM חוכמה

σοφία WISDOM חוכמה

Chapter 12.

*The king addresses his praise or complaint to god directly,
Wisdom having vacated the way of the wanderer.*

> O how good and sweet is your spirit,
> O God, in all things you inhabit!
> For you may chastise them that err,
> By little and little as they wander:
> You admonish them, and speak to them,
> Approaching with a soft voice you come,
> Whisp'ring things wherein they offend:
> That, leaving their wickedness behind,
> They may believe in you, O God,
> And follow the path whereon you tread.
>
> Those ancient peoples of your land
> You did abhor and seek to supplant,
> Because they followed in hateful ways,
> With sorceries, wicked sacrifices,
> Merciless murder of their own children,
> Eaters of bowels and blood therein.
> There in the midst of your holy land,

σοφία　　WISDOM　　חוכמה

They sacrificed with their own hands
Their own children, helpless souls,
And thus it came to be your will
These iniquitous souls to kill,
Destroyed by the hands of the just, withal,
That the land, this land, which of them all
Is held most dearly in your right hand,
Might then belong to children of God.

Yet all who lived there, in this place,
Both the just and the iniquitous,
Suffered the pain of wasps you sent,
Made little by little penitent.
You could have made the wicked and just
All suffer death by war, or beast,
Or by your power, destroyed at once;
But made your judgments by degrees:
You gave them many miseries,
Then found them places to repent,
Full knowing they were ignorant,
That they were a wicked generation,

σοφία   WISDOM   חוכמה

Their malice a natural condition,
And that what they were believing
Could not escape their self-deceiving.
Their seed was cursed from the beginning:
But God does not fear the one sinning.

Who says to God: What have you done?
Who shall withstand God's judgment then?
Who comes at God to avenge the wicked?
Who shall accuse God, if they are dead?

God makes the nation, God the death,
God makes the air and takes the breath.

There is no other God but you,
Who cares for all they say and do;
They have no standing to make claim
That God has been unfair to them.

Neither shall king, nor tyrant decry
All those who may in a battle die.

σοφία WISDOM חוכמה

For in this matter you are just,
Things happen there as right they must:
God's power is never congruent
With punishing the innocent.
God's power, of justice is the seed:
We cannot by ourselves abide;
Because you are the God of all,
Your gracious power must judge us well.
When people forget what you can do
You find a deed of power to show,
Thus to convince the deluded mind
Of those that to your power are blind.

But you judge with tranquility;
And with favor show us the way:
For your power is apposite
When we are most in need of it.

By such works you have taught us, God,
We must be just and strive for good,
A cause for hope you give your children:

σοφία WISDOM חוכמה

Because, in judging what they have done,
You give place to repent their sin.
You killed the enemies of your people,
(And they deserved to die, withal)
But with so great deliberation,
Giving them time for absolution,
And place whereby they might yet move
To change their wickedness to love.

O God, how circumspect your view
In judging your own children so;
From long before made covenant,
And from all harshness did relent.
Therefore whereas you chastise us,
You scourge our foes so many ways,
To the end that when we judge you
We may think on your goodness, too:
And when we are judged after we die,
We may truly hope for mercy;
For as justice is tempered by mercy,
So also may mercy take the first place,

σοφία   WISDOM   חוכמה

And thereafter be tempered by justice.
However, you also greatly torment
Those whose lives, so foolishly spent,
Unjustly honored mindless things
Which they worshipped with offerings.
For they went astray for a long time
And in the way of error found home,
Treating as gods those things which are
Worthless for beast or human creature,
Living like children without a care.
Therefore you judge them heedless children,
Scold them, yet show them how to amend.
Those not amended by mockery's rod
Feel yet more worthy judgment from God.
For seeing that they have suffered by
Those very things that led them astray,
When these their sins did them betray,
They acknowledged that God was true,
Whom in time past they did not know:
Which ended their condemnation also.

Ω

σοφία   W I S D O M   חוכמה

Chapter 13.

The king engages in musings about how the nations choose their gods, and disparages gods made by hand.

All are vain, in whom is a void,

Where there is no knowledge of God:

And who by these good things we see

Could not discern how God could be;

Neither attending to sacred book,

Nor telling whose was the handiwork:

Instead imagining, either the fire,

The wind, the circle of stars, the swift air,

The great wide water, the sun and moon,

To be the gods that make earth turn.

If they delight in all the beauty,

Which they took as a deity,

Let them know now by how much more

Our God is more than their gods are:

For the first creator of this beauty

Made all those things beautifully.

Or if they admired the visible powers

In the effects of these vast creatures,

σοφία   WISDOM   חוכמה

Let their understanding of time,
The cause and effect of what may come,
Be proof that God has made them this way,
And that God is mightier than they.

For by the greatness of the beauty,
And strength of the creature on display,
The creator of them may be seen,
And thereby also may be known.
Many kinds of human are named;
Perhaps some are more to be blamed,
For they may err, as they seek God,
Yet fail to say what wrong they did.
Knowing these works, they search for cause,
And seek to extract some perfect laws,
And are persuaded some things are good
Not seeking whence they might proceed;
But even these souls are not to be pardoned.
For if they could discern so well
(Enough to judge with certainty the small,)
How did they not then see the God,

σοφία   WISDOM   חוכמה

The only God, and all that God did?

Sorry are they, by reason only led,
Their only living hope among the dead;
They have called gods, works of human hand,
Wrought with an art that few can understand,
Bought with gold and silver, sequestered fast,
Fearful in their resemblance to a beast,
Or curious stonework of an ancient past.

It is as if an artist, once a carpenter,
Has taken down a tree as he sees proper,
Touched and hefted the wood unworked,
Skillfully taken off all the bark,
And then, with art, formed him a vessel
Fit for the common use of a household;
Then saves the wood chips and shaving
To dress the meat for dinner that evening.
He saves what's left, a twisted part,
Which is otherwise good for nought,
Being crooked, and full of knots,

σοφία WISDOM חכמה

Carves diligently in idle moments,
When there is nothing else to do,
By skill of art shapes one end so,
To make the image of a crow;
Or other face of man or beast;
Laying it over with vermillion paste,
Painting it red, filling a spot
That mars the appearance of the coat.
Then he makes a safe dwelling place
Where the small effigy finds a house,
He sets it in a wall, a niche,
With a white candle on a dish,
He fastens it with an iron patch,
Mounts a small door with clever latch,
Providing for it, lest it should fall,
Knowing it cannot stay at will:
For it is just an effigy,
And has some need of help, to stay.
Then the artist makes prayer to it,
Inquires, what food the household will eat,
Seeks marriage, children, happiness, the lot.

σοφία   WISDOM   חוכמה

This person is not ashamed to speak
To that which has no life, no spark.
Such souls for health make supplication
To the weak force of superstition;
Such souls pray for life, to the dead,
Make ritual marks on face and head;
For understanding they seek sooth-sayers,
Transforming money to answered prayers.
For a safe journey they petition a doll,
That cannot walk, in the niche on the wall:
For getting more, for working less,
For a proper outcome if neighbors transgress,
The artist of wood will ask the thing
That is unable to do anything.

Ω

σοφία WISDOM חוכמה

σοφία   WISDOM   חוכמה

Chapter 14.

*Showing the insufficiency of wrought gods and images,
and how worship of them leads to corruption and injustice.*

> Again, another designs to sail;
> Beginning some project the soul craves,
> To lead a voyage through raging waves,
> Calls upon pieces of wood more frail
> Than the fleshy wood that carries the soul.
> For this, a desire for gain devised,
> And the workman's skill was realized.
>
> Your providence, God, governs the whole:
> For you make a way in the ocean's roll,
> You find sure paths among the waves,
> In storm, O God, 'tis your hand that saves:
> You save out of all things, ev'ry part,
> Even a sailor at sea without art.
> But that the works of your people
> Might not be idle, you send storm:
> And knowing this, people trust their lives
> To a little wood, upon great waves.

σοφία WISDOM חוכמה

Passing them over the sea, you save,
And they do not taste a watery grave.
And from the beginning of the world,
When the proud giants perished and fell,
The hope of the world fled to an ark,
Which rose upon the waters dark,
And was governed by your great hand,
Seeking a shore in an unknown land
Where human seed might once more stand.

For blessèd the wood which brings justice,
Under the guidance of judgment's eyes;
But the idol made by hands is a curse,
And they that made it are yet worse:
They, because of the thing they did;
And it, being frail, being called a god.

But God does not this distinction make,
Wicked and wickedness are hateful alike.
And that which is made, suffers torments,
With those that shaped it in their hands.

σοφία   WISDOM   חוכמה

Therefore there shall be no protection
For idols of another nation:
Because with the device of thought,
These things, however finely wrought,
Are turned to an abomination,
And for the soul a rank temptation,
A snare that catches the unwise,
A tightening of religion's vise.

For the beginning of fornication
Is devising idols and prostration:
The invention of them and their purveyors
Mingle corruption with our prayers.
For they were not from the beginning there,
And neither shall they be for ever.
By vanity of human thought
They came before us, and they were bought:
And in time's fullness shall be found
To find decay within the ground.
A father suffers with bitter grief,
Makes an image of his son, alive,

σοφία   WISDOM   חוכמה

The son who was, to all, heav'ns ray;
Was terribly, quickly, taken away:
The son had died as a young man,
But thus the father now began
To worship the image as a god.
Informing his servants of what he did,
He appoints rites and sacrifices,
And daily performance of services.

Likewise a woman makes an image
When her daughter dies at young age.

And then a wicked custom prevailed,
This error, made law, was kept and held,
By fathers and mothers throughout the land,
Statues were worshipped by command,
Placed along streets by a tyrant's hand;
Then came the time when the emperor
Said he was god and commanded favor,
So those at court, so far away,
Whom people of God could not reach to pray,

σοφία   WISDOM   חוכמה

> Nor worship in presence, for they dwelt afar,
> Now brought resemblances to the square,
> Made many an image of the one
> Whom they had such a mind to honor:
> And so that people might touch this one,
> Have the face pressed into their coin.
> That by this, their great diligence,
> And to obliterate all good sense,
> The people might honor as present,
> The erstwhile god-king that was absent.
>
> To ease the worshipping of these,
> The vigorous energies of the artificer
> Brought forward crowds of the ignorant,
> Making false worship more permanent.
> For the artisan, seeking more income,
> Willing to please an employer's whim,
> Put aside his own ethical belief,
> And labored all the hours of his life,
> With all known art to make that face
> That all beheld in every place.

σοφία   WISDOM   חוכמה

And the multitude, carried away
By all this beauty on display,
Took the facsimile now for a god
That just a little before was heard
To be a man who practised reason
And, perhaps, was a good person.

And so did occasion arrive
For deceiving of human life:
When people, serving esthetic taste,
Or rulers, prone to laying waste,
First gave the incommunicable name
To stones and wood and captive flame.
And it was not enough they had
Erred about the knowledge of God:
They also live midst a great war,
Where ignorance and knowledge spar,
Yet, thinking therefore just as they please,
Call many and so great evils, peace.

For either their own children suffice

σοφία WISDOM חוכמה

To offer up for sacrifice,
Or they conjure a hidden device,
Keep late watches filled with madness,
Supplanting all the ancient observance;
So now they neither keep life pure,
Nor is their marriage undefiled.
One kills another, through envy,
One grieves another, by adultery:
And thus all things are mingled together,
Theft and dissimulation, blood, murder,
Corruption and unfaithfulness,
Tumults and perjury, arson, lies,
Disquieting of the good, false witness,
Forgetting God, defiling souls,
Changing nature, domestic abuse,
Irregularity of adultery, uncleanness,
Bastard children, venereal disease.

So, worship of abominable idols
Is cause, beginning, and end of all evils.
Either they're mad when they are merry;

σοφία WISDOM חוכמה

Or prophesy lies; or live unjustly;
Or they too easily forswear themselves.
For whilst they trust in those dead idols,
Though they sincerely swear, but falsely,
They look not to find hurt this way;
But they shall be justly punished,
Because 'tis God they have dismissed,
Gave heed to idols, made meanings twist,
And sought by guile to despise justice.

For not the idols, by whom they swear,
But penitence of sinners they should fear;
God punishes transgressions of the unjust;
The sin with the punishment is bound fast.

Ω

σοφία   WISDOM   חוכמה

Chapter 15.

On how worship of a living and forgiving god is superior to seeking justice from the dead gods of other nations.

But you, our God, are gracious, true,

Patient, merciful in all things you do.

For if we sin, we know we are yours,

We know your tolerance forgives errors.

And if we sin not, we know that we

Are counted with you eternally.

For to know God is perfect justice:

And to know perfect justice is

The root of immortality.

We are secure eternally.

For the pernicious invention

Of malicious imagination

Has not turned us away from you;

Nor will a picture fraught with shadow,

A fruitless labor, a graven figure,

Showing a face embellished in color,

The sight whereof entices fools

To lust for scent, thin cloth, and jewels,

σοφία   WISDOM   חוכמה

Imagined lust for a lifeless figure,
A still, dead image sketched on paper.
Lovers of evil things deserve
To have no better things to love:
They that make them, they that love them,
And they that worship where they come from.
The potter mixes the soft earth well,
With labor fashions every vessel,
And of the same clay makes them all,
Those that are made for clean uses,
And those that are for unclean uses;
But for what purpose a vessel is,
The potter is the judge, and says.

Of the same clay by a vain labor,
The potter makes a god-figure:
The potter, indeed, was first a ball
Of earth, inhabited by a soul,
Which will, after some little time
Return to the same earth whence it came,
When the quick life which God has lent

σοφία   WISDOM   חוכמה

Is called back, and its days are spent.
This figure's care, that the potter made,
Is not that there be work to do,
Nor that its life is short, or slow;
It strives against the other earths,
Worked by gold-and-silversmiths,
Endeavoring to shine, and gleam
As works in brass or copper gleam,
Finding its glory above all things
In stroking the vanity of kings.

The heart is ash, and hope, vain earth,
We struggle upward into birth,
Yet this life is more base than clay:
If we know not a righteous way.

Forasmuch as these smiths knew not
Their maker, that had them begot,
The God that had inspired the soul;
That works, and through their hands makes all;
That breathes into them living spirit

σοφία WISDOM חוכמה

And would divert them from the great pit;
They have counted our life a pastime,
And the business of life as gain,
That we must get, get, held in thrall,
All, all to make money from evil.

The persons who live this life of a cur,
Knowing what offends above all other,
Of earthly matter make brittle vessels,
To serve the enemies of their peoples.
Their graven gods, their aspiration,
They make these for their own subjection,
Unhappy, yet proud of them all:
For as they esteem all these idols,
The gods of heathens are also theirs,
Which also have no eyes to see,
Nor noses to sniff, nor ears to hear,
Nor the fingers of hands to handle,
And as for their feet, are slow to walk.
These persons themselves are like dumb idols,
As if they were made by other fingers;

σοφία WISDOM חוכמה

Who borrowed their own breath to make them.
For no one can make a god's visage,
That is like to a human image.

For being mortal, they form a shape,
A dead thing made in a slippery grip.
They are better than what they make,
(For their own soul's amendment's sake);
Because these artisans have lived,
Though they were mortal, they might be saved,
But this, the fashioned thing, never was.
The artisan worships vile creatures:
But compared to them, beings without sense
Are worse, and never know God's embrace.
Yea, neither by sight can any one see
Good in an absence of humanity.
For they have no means to praise God,
And no way to express their gratitude.

Ω

σοφία   WISDOM   חוכמה

σοφία   WISDOM   חוכמה

Chapter 16.

On how these and other disagreements over gods
corrupted with violence the king's nation and their enemies.

    For making these graven images,
    And many other things likewise,
    The artisans in earths were punished,
    Destroyed by beastliness, and banished.
    God, you dealt well with your own people:
    Instead of punishment, in their trial,
    You gave them their fill of food to eat,
    Preparing quails for them, for their meat:
    To the end that they wanted this food
    Rejecting that which they formerly had,
    Which led them to loathe that which was
    Needful for survival in the past.
    After suffering momentary want,
    The people accepted either meat.
    Because they needed to continue
    Destruction of their unjust enemy
    That had sought to impose tyranny:

σοφία WISDOM חוכמה

In appeasing their thirst for blood
God gave them example, and showed
How an enemy should be destroyed.

So then God's people, with a fierce rage,
Mingling their anger and their courage,
Killed their foes with frenzied intent,
As with the bitings of a crooked serpent.
When God's anger came to relent;
They were troubled but a moment,
And then, to assure their correction,
God sent a sign of salvation
To foster remembrance and awe
For the commandments of the law.
Yet, even they that turned to it,
Were not healed by the sight of it,
But by you, God, Savior of all.

You delivered the battlefield from evil,
And in this you showed our enemies,
That you are the one who saves us.

σοφία   WISDOM   חוכמה

For the biting of locusts and flies
Devoured the dead where he now lies;
There was no remedy for his wound:
For he deserved the lot he found.
But the tooth of the venomous serpents
Spared your children; they earned repentance;
Their wounds healed, by God's own mercy;
And they live on until this day.
O Lord, you searched the warriors' mind
For the remembrance of your word,
And they were quickly healed, lest sliding
Into a deep forgetfulness, or hiding,
They might not find your healing help.
It was not herb that roused them up,
Nor mollifying plaster healed,
But your word, God, which all things willed.

For it is only you, Lord God,
That has pow'r o'er the living and dead,
To gates of death you lead them down,
And sometimes bring them back again:

σοφία   WISDOM   חוכמה

Humans indeed kill through malice,
And when the living spirit passes,
The killer hears not back again;
Neither shall any call back again
From where that soul may chance to land;
But no soul ever escapes your hand.

For the wicked were scourged by you,
By strength of your arm they were laid low,
Persecuted by strange waters,
Battered by hail, blasted by weathers;
And in the end consumed by fire,
Black smoke ascending like a spire.

And which was yet more wonderful,
In water, which extinguishes all,
The fire of God had yet more force:
For the elements fight for the just.
At the outset, the fire was low,
So that the beasts you sent might go
Strong up against the wicked line,

σοφία   WISDOM   חוכמה

And as they went, they might not burn;
But that the enemy might see
These beasts were saved miraculously;
That the unjust would come to die
Under judgment of God's own eye.

At yet another time the fire,
Surpassed itself its own hot pow'r,
Burned in the midst of the water's span,
To spoil the fruits of a wicked land.

And while the enemy was so tried,
With food of angels your people you fed:
And gave them bread from heav'n to eat,
Laid it before them at their feet;
Having within it all that is best,
And the sweetness of every taste.

For your sustenance was made whole,
Showing your sweetness to every soul,
Pleasing the will of every one,

σοφία WISDOM חוכמה

So what each wanted, that was done.
Snow and ice endured the fire,
And did not melt or soften there:
That they who saw that fire might know
There in the rain, that God's pure law
Burning away the hail and ice
Destroyed their unjust enemies.

But by this same mysterious power,
In a long year or in an hour,
God wills that the just be nourishèd,
And have no need for show of strength.

For the fire is a creature of God
Serving you the Creator, when bid;
Made fierce to arouse the impertinent,
For the unjust, their just punishment;
Fire abates its own strength away,
To soothe the ones that trust in thee.

Therefore even in these great wars,

σοφία WISDOM חוכמה

Fire transformed to other creatures,
And was obedient to your grace
That nourishes all in righteousness;
According to the will of those
Who desired assistance from you.
These your children, God, now know
Better how they must strive and grow;
It's not the growing of fruits on trees
That nourishes us in mortal ways:
But rather, your word and what you do
Preserves the ones that believe in you:

For that which is not touched by fire,
Warmed with a sunbeam, melts away:

That this truth might be known to all,
Would that we could stop the sun's ball,
To bless you, and adore you aright,
At the pure dawning of the light,
And unthankful hope shall melt away
As winter ice on a spring day. Ω

σοφία WISDOM חוכמה

σοφία   WISDOM   חוכמה

Chapter 17.

*On the fearful ways the unjust were punished for their errors,
by necessary consequence of their own sinful behavior.*

> For your judgments are great, O God,
> Yet your words cannot be expressed:
> And therefore undisciplined souls
> Have erred and wandered from your ways.
> For while the wicked in their pride
> Thought to stand firm against our side,
> And to have comfortable dominion
> Over God and God's holy nation,
> They fettered themselves more and less,
> With self-wrought bonds of iron darkness,
> And through the long night, hid their faces,
> And closed themselves inside their houses;
> Dark they lay, exiled from providence,
> In the slow canker of obscure sins;
> And while they thought so to lie hid,
> Many died rigid on their beds,
> Scattered under the darkest veil
> Of forgetfulness; piecemeal, yet full.

σοφία WISDOM חוכמה

They were all sore afraid and sick,
Staring wide of eye in the dark,
At the silent, recurrent shock
Of a knock waiting for the next knock;
The warmth and darkness where they gather,
Does not keep them from any fear:
Noises coming down trouble them,
Sad, floating visions appear to them,
There is no ending of their affright.
No power of fire can give them light,
The brightest flames the stars have lit
Cannot enlighten that voiceless night.

Then there appeared to them, sudden fire;
All of them were struck with a fear:
A face, in darkness, which was not seen,
Hidden by other things which they saw,
And which filled them with a worse awe:
And their delusions of magic art
Were put down, laid by, made no part.
And their boasting of spurious knowledge

σοφία WISDOM חוכמה

Rebuked by sound of a silent pledge,
For they who had promised to drive away
Fears, from the sick soul's troubled way,
Were sick themselves with a nameless fear
Eyes frozen in a rigid stare.
No terrible thing disturbed their rest:
Yet with the passing by of beasts,
And constant soft hissing of serpents,
Their pounding hearts beat them to death;
They lost the power to draw their breath:
Denying what they saw in the air,
More real, because it was not there.

Wickedness brings fearful commotion,
Bears witness to its own condemnation:
For the troubled conscience of kings
Always forecasts grievous things.
Fear offers nothing to be taught
But yielding up the succour of thought.

And while there is small expectation

σοφία WISDOM חוכמה

That we may find some consolation
From there inside thought's habitation,
So greater will be the ignorance
Of that cause which our soul torments;
The fear we might have, thus displaced,
By cravings for our Maker's face.
But they that died in that dark night,
Found nothing could remove from sight
The visible fears that plagued them all,
Sent from the lowest and deepest hell:
At the end, they slept the same sleep;
And after, were buried just as deep.
Sometimes molested with the fear
Of monsters, chasing near and far;
Sometimes fainting straight away,
Souls failing, collapsing suddenly;
That deadly sudden, intrusive fear
Would not come at them any more.
If any of them had fallen then,
Their souls would be kept shut within
A prison without chain or iron.

σοφία   WISDOM   חוכמה

If any one were a husbandman,
A shepherd, or laborer on the plain,
And this one suddenly overtaken,
He would endure the necessity,
A task from which he could not fly.

For they were all bound up together
With one chain of darkness, one tether.
Whether it were a whistling wind,
The melodious voice of birds in blend
Among the spreading branches of trees,
Or a great fall of water sprays,
Running down with loud violence,
Or the mightier noise of stones
Tumbling down sides of mountains,
Or the running force unseen
Of beasts at play in forest green,
Or yet, the roaring voice of beasts,
And the rebounding echo's blast
Against the highest mountainside:

σοφία WISDOM חוכמה

These noises, wrought by godless pride,
Made them to swoon from fear inside.

For the whole world was filled with light,
And none were hindered from seeing it;
Safe at home or with their neighbors,
In their rest or in their labors:

They might have found it with delight:
But over them only was spread night,
An image of darkness, heavy with threat,
Of that which was to come upon them:
They were to themselves as a dream
Darker than darkness, yet to come.

Ω

σοφία   WISDOM   חוכמה

Chapter 18.

A justification for the dreadful punishment of the enemies of those who would claim to be the children of god.

But your saints lived in a great light,
They heard their own voices in the night,
Although their shapes were vague and dim
They did not suffer from beast or dream,
They glorified and thanked their God
For every thing they saw and did.
And they that before had been wronged,
Gave thanks, for their lives were prolonged,
And asked this gift, this recompense,
That each of them might make a difference.

Therefore God gave a pillar of fire
To guide the weary wanderer;
And God gave them a harmless sun
To measure them their daily round.
The unjust, those who died in the night,
Deserved to be deprived of light,

σοφία   WISDOM   חוכמה

They sat in darkness, locked away,
No longer touched by the sun's ray,
Remembering their evil deed
How they enslaved the children of God,
By whom the pure light of the law
Came on us, and all people saw.
And now in darkness they dimly see,
The justice God makes them obey:
Whereas they thought it child's play
To murder every firstborn boy;
(One child before this being released,
And saved, in semblance of the good);
But you took vengeance on them, God:
You took away a multitude,
And you destroyed them all together
In a mighty raging water.

That night was endured, long before,
And remembered by our ancestors,
That knowing what oaths they trusted to,
They might have courage in what they do.

σοφία   WISDOM   חוכמה

So God, your people received from you
Eternal salvation of the just,
And saw destruction of the unjust.

For as you punished our adversaries,
You also encouraged and glorified us.
For the just children of good people
Were offering sacrifice secretly,
And every one of them called on you
To foster justice in what they do:
That just people should always make
A place for both good and evil alike,
Singing now the praise of God,
The father, the mother, and the child.

But from the unjust women and men,
There sounded an endless outcry then,
A lamentable mourning was heard
For all the children that had died,
For the servant who suffered the same

σοφία WISDOM חוכמה

As the master who oversaw him,
And for the common man standing by
Who suffered just as the authority.
So all alike, the innumerable dead,
With one death they might be buried.
There were not enough living to bury them;
None to speak words and reverence them;
For in one moment, as there they stood,
Both base and noble of them died.
For whereas they would not believe
Anything, before that instant arrived,
Because they obscured reason with charms,
And sought enchantments to ward off harms;
Then, at the destruction of the firstborn,
They saw their own slaves to be of God,
And God the master of every deed.
And while all things still were in silence,
And the night in the midst of her course,
The word of God leapt down from heaven,
A force descending from a throne,
As a fierce conqueror you came,

σοφία   WISDOM   חוכמה

Into the midst of that land of doom,
A sharp sword carried your great command,
God stood, and death sprang from God's hand,
And there on earth as God did stand
Fire rose to heaven from the land.

Sudden visions of evil dreams
Troubled the sleepers in their rooms;
Sudden fears came over them
Before the morning light had come.

One still, another gasping for breath,
Half dead, or showing the cause of death.
The flickering visions that troubled them
Foreshadowed things they knew would come,
As if God would not let them perish
Without knowing their last desperate wish.

God afterwards visited the just
With an assault of death in the dust;
There was surely a deadly loss

σοφία WISDOM חוכמה

Of those people in the wilderness:
But God, your wrath did not continue;
Most of your people, you let go.
For if a blameless person will
Make haste to pray for all the people,
Bringing forth this shield of prayer,
This call for what is just and fair,
By incense, making supplication;
Withstanding God's wrath, and our damnation,
It makes end to the calamity,
By showing one servant's purity;
This one defended all the rest,
Not by strength of body or fist,
Nor with the force of arms or sword,
But subdued him with a mere word,
The one who sought to punish them;
Calling on oaths to protect him,
Covenants with those who had died.

For when they were all fallen down dead

σοφία   WISDOM   חוכמה

    By heaps upon one another's head,

    This one stood fast to protect the others;
    Dead as they were and piled together,
    He stayed the assault against his brothers.
    For in the priestly garment he wore,
    Was the whole world in miniature:
    And in the four rows of the stones
    The glory of all ages graven,
    And your majesty so written,
    Upon his head the diadem was,
    To these the defender gave a place,
    He feared them as he did God's face,
    Proof of God's wrath secured his praise.

Ω

σοφία WISDOM חוכמה

σοφία   WISDOM   חוכמה

Chapter 19.

The king's claims, in the absence of Wisdom, concerning the last disposition of his nation and their defeated enemies.

To the wicked, at the end, came

Wrath without mercy, in God's name.

The people's Savior before this, knew

Exactly what things they would do:

For when they gave us leave to depart,

And had sent us away with good heart,

They changed their mind, and chased us down.

For whilst they were yet in mourning,

Lamenting at the graves of their lost,

They took up another foolish device:

And pursued us as fugitives

Whom before they had pressed to leave.

For a well-deserved necessity,

Of which they were quite worthy,

Brought them to this fearful end:

They lost remembrance of what had happened,

That the search for their own punishment

σοφία   WISDOM   חוכמה

Might fill the void in their torments:
That we God's people, might pass through,
But they might find a new way to die.

For every creature according to its kind
Was fashioned again as from the beginning,
Seeking, and obeying, your commandment,
And your children kept without ailment.
A cloud overshadowed the land,
And where water was before, dry land;
And there, where the Red Sea was,
A way without hindrance for us;
And out of the great deep, safe passage,
Through which all the nation passed,
Safely protected by your hand,
Treading the newly formed dry land,
Seeing your miracle run its courses.
For they fed on their food like horses,
And they skipped about like lambs,
For you God, who had delivered them.
For they were mindful of how they had come,

σοφία WISDOM חוכמה

All that had been done in the desert:
How the ground brought forth flies from dirt,
How cattle and sheep died in the heat,
And how the river cast up a multitude,
Not fishes but croaking frogs instead.
The hungry wanderers saw go by
A migrating flock of birds in the sky;
Tormented by their appetite,
They dreamed in the night of delicate meat.
As if to satisfy their desire,
Quail came up to them from the water.
Punishments came upon the sinners,
But never without foreshadowing signs:
The force of thunder in the hot air,
And a night of a thousand falling stars.
Their suffering measured, more and less,
According to their own wickedness.
For the unjust sinners came to pay
For detestable inhospitality:
Others indeed received not strangers
Repelling those unknown to them;

σοφία WISDOM חוכמה

But some brought their guests into the home,
That had deserved so well of them;
Then gave them bondage, and not only so,
But in another respect also,
They were worse than being hostile;
For some others against their will
Received strangers who to them came,
But then grievously afflicted them
Whom they had received with joy,
And who lived in just the same way.

But the unjust were struck with blindness:
Approaching the doors of the just,
They were covered with sudden darkness,
And every one sought to return
Back through the door where he came in.

For just as the notes of a familiar song
May be changed, either right or wrong,
As when an instrument will play,
The listener feels a change in gravity,

σοφία WISDOM חוכמה

Yet the tune has its path preserved:
All this may clearly be perceived
By the way we recognize the song,
Even as it passes through change.
For many things that had lived on land
Were turned into things of the water:
And things that before swam in the water
Passed out of it onto the land.
Fire had power in water above its own virtue,
And the water forgot its quenching nature.
But then for a while fire was no longer hot;
And the flesh of animals in flame, wasted not.

So by whatever way you move,
In all things you expressed your love;
Whether or not your way was understood,
You magnified your faithful people, God.
You honored, and did not despise them,
But helped in every place and every time.

Ω

σοφία WISDOM חוכמה

σοφία   WISDOM   חוכמה

Afterword.

Well, I hope all you folks are feeling just a little wiser now, than you were before you read through this book. The world needs all the wisdom it can get, for the following reason: when people work and slave to overcome injustice, superstition, ignorance and all those other malice-laden things, they may actually succeed in their efforts; but the unjust leave behind templates. The defensive mechanism which held the injustice, legitimized it, concealed it, twisted the preventive laws or the injustice itself to make it available but not visible: these intentional distortions are still there, waiting for another crime to come and inhabit their friendly niche of concealment, and this time without even having to go through the labor of creating and ingenuity of applying the original prevarications.

The root of all evil is not money, per se, but rather intentional lying and dissimulation. That is, false witness, and not pride, is the crown of all the other sins. The proof of this is that it is a natural (and usually unobjectionable) human trait to conceal guilt of any sin (especially adultery or murder) by lying about it. Remember, every moment that goes by without the sinner 'fessing up is actually a reiteration of the same lies, even if we choose to leave aside the time and effort spent on manufacturing such alternative scenarios.

And the seemingly perfect, sinless illusion which human beings create to account for themselves, gradually transforms into something both unchangeable and seemingly godlike. We strike a devil's bargain, inviting the forces of craft, technology, ingenuity, economic return, and power, to satisfy our urges for creation of false gods within us. In our self-empowerment we make stories and simulacra about human matters, and eventually try our hands at making synthetic human beings. In our own eyes, we seem to become gods.

Made in the USA
Middletown, DE
29 September 2019